WIND SONG

WIND SONG

CARL SANDBURG

Illustrated by William A. Smith

HARCOURT, BRACE AND COMPANY, NEW YORK

To John Carl and Karlen Paula

Dear young folks:

Some poems may please you for
half a minute & you don't care
whether you keep them or not.
Other poems you may feel to be
priceless & you hug them to your
heart & keep them for sure.
Here in this book poems of each
kind may be found: you do the finding.
   I sign this book for you
saying love & blessings: may luck
stars ever be over you.

                    Carl Sandburg

CONTENTS

LITTLE ALBUM

CORN BELT

NIGHT

BLOSSOM THEMES

WIND, SEA, AND SKY

WIND SONG

NEW POEMS

BLUEBIRD, WHAT DO YOU FEED ON?

Bluebird, what do you feed on?
It is true you gobble up worms, you
    swallow bugs,
And your bill picks up corn, seed,
    berries.
This is only part of the answer.
Your feathers have captured a piece of
    smooth sky.
Your wings are burnished with
    lake-morning blue.
It is not a worm blue nor a bug
    blue nor the blue
Of corn or berry you shine with.
Bluebird, we come to you for facts,
    for valuable
Information, for secret reports.
Bluebird, tell us, what do you
    feed on?

NEVER TWO SONGS THE SAME

the light on the leaves
in girlish early spring
  the deep green of the matron leaves
  in the stride of high summer suns
the colors of the turning oak and maple
when October crosses gold and brown
  there is winter then to wait for
  when trees wear frost of a morning
      wear snow of an evening
  when bare branches often reach out
  saying they would be lonely
  only for the wind coming
  with never two songs the same
  with changes always in the old songs

DAYBREAK

Daybreak comes first
   in thin splinters shimmering.
Neither is the day here
   nor is the night gone.
Night is getting ready to go
And Day whispers, "Soon now, soon."

BEE SONG

Bees in the late summer sun
Drone their song
Of yellow moons
Trimming black velvet,
Droning, droning a sleepysong.

BUBBLES

Two bubbles found they had rainbows on their curves.
They flickered out saying:
"It was worth being a bubble just to have held that
rainbow thirty seconds."

in the old deep sing-song of the sea
in the old going-on of that sing-song
in that old mama-mama-mama going-on
of that nightlong daylong sleepsong
we look on   we listen
we lay by and hear
too many big bells   too many long gongs
too many weepers over a lost gone gold
too many laughs over light green gold
woven and changing in the wash and the heave
moving on the bottoms   winding in the waters
sending themselves with arms and voices
up in the old mama-mama-mama music
up into the whirl of spokes of light

The little boat at anchor
in black water sat murmuring
to the tall black sky.

***

A white sky bomb fizzed on a black line.
A rocket hissed its red signature into the west.
Now a shower of Chinese fire alphabets,
a cry of flower pots broken in flames,
a long curve to a purple spray,
three violet balloons—

Drips of seaweed tangled in gold,
shimmering symbols of mixed numbers,
tremulous arrangements of cream gold folds
of a bride's wedding gown—

***

A few sky bombs spoke their pieces,
then velvet dark.

The little boat at anchor
in black water sat murmuring
to the tall black sky.

SEA WISDOM

The sea was always the sea
and a maker was the sea always.
What the sea was making you may know
by asking the sea and getting an answer.
Well the sea knows its own importance.
Well the sea will answer you when it knows
                              your importance.

NIGHTSONG

bring me now the bright flower
of the moongold grass—
let me have later on the horizon
the black gold of moonset—
spill for me then the bowl of dawn
overshot and streaming—
for men have often seen and taken
night as a changing scene
priceless yet paid for

PORTRAIT OF A CHILD SETTLING DOWN FOR
AN AFTERNOON NAP

Marquita had blossom fists
   and bubble toes.
I saw them, touched them,
the same as an oak gnarled and worn
when the wind bends it down
to a frail hope of an oak
and their leaves touch
and branch whispers to branch.

"Baby say blossom for you are a blossom,
Baby say bubble for you are a bubble,"
   I said to Marquita.
And as she lay ready
and prepared to spit at the sky,
I told her to spit in the face of the wind,
not yet having learned what happens.

   San Francisco lay in silver tones
   and the Golden Gate swaddled
   in frames of blue mountains
while Marquita lay swathed as a sweet pig,
pink as a fresh independent pig
         ready to spit at the sky.

STARS

The stars are too many to count.
The stars make sixes and sevens.
The stars tell nothing—and everything.
The stars look scattered.
Stars are so far away they never speak
    when spoken to.

BE READY

Be land ready
for you shall go back to land.

Be sea ready
for you have been nine-tenths water
and the salt taste shall cling to your mouth.

Be sky ready
for air, air, has been so needful to you—
you shall go back, back to the sky.

Now I go down here and bring up a moon.
How much am I bid for the moon?
You see it a bright moon and brand-new.
What can I get to start it?   how much?
What! who ever ever heard such a bid for a moon?
   Come now, gentlemen, come.
This is a solid guaranteed moon.
You may never have another chance
   to make a bid on such a compact
   eighteen-carat durable gold moon.
You could shape a thousand wedding rings
   out of this moongold.
I can guarantee the gold and the weddings
   will last forever
   and then a thousand years more.
Come gentlemen, no nonsense, make me a bid.

SLEEP SONG

Into any little room
may come a tall steel bridge
and a long white fog,
changing lights and mist,
moving as if a great sea
and many mighty waters
had come into that room
easy with bundles of sleep,
bundles of sea-moss sheen,
shapes of sunset cunning,
shifts of moonrise gold—
   slow talk of low fog
   on your forehead,
   hands of cool fog
   on your eyes—
so let a sleep song be spoken—
let spoken fog sheets come
out of a long white harbor—
let a slow mist deliver
long bundles of sleep.

ALICE CORBIN IS GONE

Alice Corbin is gone
and the Indians tell us where.
   She trusted the Indians
   and they kept a trust in her.
She took a four-line Indian song
   and put it into English.
You can sing it over and over:

The wind is carrying me round the sky;
The wind is carrying me round the sky.
   My body is here in the valley—
The wind is carrying me round the sky.

LINES WRITTEN FOR GENE KELLY TO
DANCE TO

Spring is when the grass turns green and glad.
Spring is when the new grass comes up and says, "Hey, hey!
    Hey, hey!"
Be dizzy now and turn your head upside down and see how
    the world looks upside down.
Be dizzy now and turn a cartwheel, and see the good earth
    through a cartwheel.

Tell your feet the alphabet.
Tell your feet the multiplication table.
Tell your feet where to go, and watch 'em go and come back.

Can you dance a question mark?
Can you dance an exclamation point?
Can you dance a couple of commas?
And bring it to a finish with a period?

Can you dance like the wind is pushing you?
Can you dance like you are pushing the wind?
Can you dance with slow wooden heels
    and then change to bright and singing silver heels?
Such nice feet, such good feet.

So long as grass grows and rivers run
Silver lakes like blue porcelain plates
Silver snakes of winding rivers.
You can see 'em on a map.

Why we got geography?

Because we go from place to place. Because the earth used to be flat and had four corners, and you could jump off from any of the corners.

But now the earth is not flat any more. Now it is round all over. Now it is a globe, a ball, round all over, and we would all fall off it and tumble away into space if it wasn't for the magnetic poles. And when you dance it is the North Pole or the South Pole pulling on your feet like magnets to keep your feet on the earth.

And that's why we got geography.

And it's nice to have it that way.

Why does duh Mississippi River wind and wind?

Why, dat's easy. She wind so she git where she wanna go.

Mississippi, Rappahannock, Punxatawney. Spell out their names with your heels.

Where duh towns uh Punxatawney and Mauk Chunk? Why, yeanh day's bof in Pennsylvan-ee-eye-ay.

And dat's why we got geography.

Left foot, tweedle-dum—right foot tweedle-dee, here they go.

When Yankee Doodle come to town, wot wuz he a-ridin' on?

A buffalo? A elephant? A horse?

No, no, no, no. A pony it wuz, a pony.

That's right—

Giddi-ap, Giddi-ap, Giddi-ap, Giddi-ap.

Whoa! Whoa!

LITTLE PEOPLE

LITTLE GIRL, BE CAREFUL WHAT YOU SAY

Little girl, be careful what you say
when you make talk with words, words—
for words are made of syllables
and syllables, child, are made of air—
and air is so thin—air is the breath of God—
air is finer than fire or mist,
finer than water or moonlight,
finer than spider-webs in the moon,
finer than water-flowers in the morning:
    and words are strong, too,
    stronger than rocks or steel
stronger than potatoes, corn, fish, cattle,
and soft, too, soft as little pigeon-eggs,
soft as the music of hummingbird wings.
    So, little girl, when you speak greetings,
when you tell jokes, make wishes or prayers,
    be careful, be careless, be careful,
    be what you wish to be.

CHILDREN OF THE DESERT
from *The People, Yes*

1.

The old timer on the desert was gray
and grizzled with ever seeing the sun:
    "For myself I don't care whether it rains.
    I've seen it rain.
    But I'd like to have it rain
    pretty soon sometime.
    Then my son could see it.
    He's never seen it rain."

2.

"What is the east? Have you been in the east?"
the New Jersey woman asked the little girl
the wee child growing up in Arizona who said:
"Yes, I've been in the east,
the east is where trees come
between you and the sky."

BUFFALO BILL

Boy heart of Johnny Jones—aching today?
Aching, and Buffalo Bill in town?
Buffalo Bill and ponies, cowboys, Indians?

Some of us know
All about it, Johnny Jones.
Buffalo Bill is a slanting look of the eyes,
    A slanting look under a hat on a horse.
He sits on a horse and a passing look is fixed
    On Johnny Jones, you and me, barelegged,
A slanting, passing, careless look under a hat on a horse.

Go clickety-clack, O pony hoofs along the street.
Come on and slant your eyes again, O Buffalo Bill.
Give us again the ache of our boy hearts.
Fill us again with the red love of prairies,
    dark nights, lonely wagons,
    and the crack-crack of rifles
    sputtering flashes into an ambush.

WE MUST BE POLITE
*(Lessons for children on how to behave under
peculiar circumstances)*

1

If we meet a gorilla
what shall we do?
Two things we may do
if we so wish to do.

Speak to the gorilla,
very, very respectfully,
"How do you do, sir?"

Or, speak to him with less
distinction of manner,
"Hey, why don't you go back
where you came from?"

2

If an elephant knocks on your door
and asks for something to eat,
there are two things to say:

Tell him there are nothing but cold
victuals in the house and he will do
better next door.

Or say: We have nothing but six bushels
of potatoes—will that be enough for
your breakfast, sir?

ARITHMETIC

Arithmetic is where numbers fly like pigeons in and out of your head.

Arithmetic tells you how many you lose or win if you know how many you had before you lost or won.

Arithmetic is seven eleven all good children go to heaven—or five six bundle of sticks.

Arithmetic is numbers you squeeze from your head to your hand to your pencil to your paper till you get the answer.

Arithmetic is where the answer is right and everything is nice and you can look out of the window and see the blue sky— or the answer is wrong and you have to start all over and try again and see how it comes out this time.

If you take a number and double it and double it again and then double it a few more times, the number gets bigger and bigger and goes higher and higher and only arithmetic can tell you what the number is when you decide to quit doubling.

Arithmetic is where you have to multiply—and you carry the multiplication table in your head and hope you won't lose it.

If you have two animal crackers, one good and one bad, and you eat one and a striped zebra with streaks all over him eats the other, how many animal crackers will you have if somebody offers you five six seven and you say No no no and you say Nay nay nay and you say Nix nix nix?

If you ask your mother for one fried egg for breakfast and she gives you two fried eggs and you eat both of them, who is better in arithmetic, you or your mother?

The bigger the box the more it holds.
Empty boxes hold the same as empty heads.
Enough small empty boxes thrown into a big empty box
    fill it full.
A half-empty box says, "Put more in."
A big enough box could hold the world.
Elephants need big boxes to hold a dozen
    elephant handkerchiefs.
Fleas fold little handkerchiefs and fix them
    nice and neat in flea handkerchief boxes.
Bags lean against each other
    and boxes stand independent.
Boxes are square with corners
    unless round with circles.
Box can be piled on box
    till the whole works come tumbling.
Pile box on box and the bottom box says,
    "If you will kindly take notice
    you will see it all rests on me."
Pile box on box and the top one says,
    "Who falls farthest if or when we fall? I ask you."
Box people go looking for boxes
    and bag people go looking for bags.

SIXTEEN MONTHS

On the lips of the child Janet float changing dreams.
It is a thin spiral of blue smoke,
A morning campfire at a mountain lake.

On the lips of the child Janet,
Wisps of haze on ten miles of corn,
Young light blue calls to young light gold of morning.

MARGARET

Many birds and the beating of wings
Make a flinging reckless hum
In the early morning at the rocks
Above the blue pool
Where the gray shadows swim lazy.

In your blue eyes, O reckless child,
I saw today many little wild wishes,
Eager as the great morning.

LAUGHING CHILD
from *Three Spring Notations on Bipeds*

The child is on my shoulders.
In the prairie moonlight the child's legs
    hang over my shoulders.
She sits on my neck and I hear her calling
    me a good horse.
She slides down—and into the moon silver of
    a prairie stream.
She throws a stone and laughs at the clug-clug.

Wendy put her black eyes on me
and swept me with her black eyes—
sweep on sweep she swept me.
    Have you ever seen Wendy?
    Have you ever seen her sweep
    Keeping her black eyes on you
    keeping you eyeswept?

The child Margaret begins to write numbers on a Saturday morning, the first numbers formed under her wishing child fingers.

All the numbers come well-born, shaped in figures assertive for a frieze in a child's room.

Both 1 and 7 are straightforward, military, filled with lunge and attack, erect in shoulder-straps.

The 6 and 9 salute as dancing sisters, elder and younger, and 2 is a trapeze actor swinging to handclaps.

All the numbers are well-born, only 3 has a hump on its back and 8 is knock-kneed.

The child Margaret kisses all once and gives two kisses to 3 and 8.

(Each number is a brand-new rag doll. . . . O in the wishing fingers . . . millions of rag dolls, millions and millions of new rag dolls!!)

PAPER I

Paper is two kinds, to write on, to wrap with.
If you like to write, you write.
If you like to wrap, you wrap.
Some papers like writers, some like wrappers.
Are you a writer or a wrapper?

I write what I know on one side of the paper
and what I don't know on the other.

Fire likes dry paper and wet paper laughs at
fire.

Empty paper sacks say, "Put something in me,
what are we waiting for?"

Paper sacks packed to the limit say, "We hope
we don't bust."

Paper people like to meet other paper people.

DOORS

An open door says, "Come in."
A shut door says, "Who are you?"
Shadows and ghosts go through shut doors.
If a door is shut and you want it shut,
    why open it?
If a door is open and you want it open,
    why shut it?
Doors forget but only doors know what it is
    doors forget.

LITTLE ALBUM

NAMES
from PROLOGUE to *The Family of Man*

There is only one horse on the earth
and his name is All Horses.
There is only one bird in the air
and his name is All Wings.
There is only one fish in the sea
and his name is All Fins.
There is only one man in the world
and his name is All Men.
There is only one woman in the world
and her name is All Women.
There is only one child in the world
and the child's name is All Children.

There is only one Maker in the world
and His children cover the earth
and they are named All God's Children.

PROVERBS
from *The People, Yes*

We'll see what we'll see.

Time is a great teacher.

Today me and tomorrow maybe you.

This old anvil laughs at many broken hammers.

What is bitter to stand against today may be sweet to remember tomorrow.

Whether the stone bumps the jug or the jug bumps the stone it is bad for the jug.

We all belong to the same big family and have the same smell.

Handling honey, tar or dung some of it sticks to the fingers.

The liar comes to believe his own lies.

He who burns himself must sit on the blisters.

God alone understands fools.

The sea has fish for every man.

Every blade of grass has its share of dew.

The longest day must have its end.

Man's life? A candle in the wind, hoar-frost on stone.

Nothing more certain than death and nothing more uncertain than the hour.

Men live like birds together in a wood; when the time comes each takes his flight.

As wave follows wave, so new men take old men's places.

HOME
from *Poems Done on a Late Night Car*

Here is a thing my heart wishes
the world had more of:
I heard it in the air of one night
when I listened to a mother
singing softly to a child
restless and angry in the darkness.

GOLDWING MOTH

A goldwing moth is between the scissors
  and the ink bottle on the desk.
Last night it flew hundreds of circles
  around a glass bulb and a flame wire.
The wings are a soft gold;
It is the gold of illuminated initials
  in manuscripts of the medieval monks.

SO TO SPEAK

Dreams, graves, pools, growing
flowers, cornfields—these are
silent, so to speak.

Northwest blizzards, sea rocks
apounding in high wind, southeast
sleet after a thaw—these are heard,
so to speak.

CIRCLES
from *The People, Yes*

The white man drew a small circle in the sand
   and told the red man,
"This is what the Indian knows,"
And drawing a big circle around the small one,
"This is what the white man knows."

The Indian took the stick
And swept an immense ring around both circles:
"This is where the white man and the red man
   know nothing."

MY PEOPLE

My people are gray,
    pigeon gray, dawn gray, storm gray.
I call them beautiful,
    and I wonder where they are going.

BASKET

Speak, sir, and be wise.
Speak choosing your words, sir,
    like an old woman over a bushel
    of apples.

HATS

Hats, where do you belong?
what is under you?

On the rim of a skyscraper's forehead
I looked down and saw: hats: fifty thousand hats:
Swarming with a noise of bees and sheep, cattle and water-
    falls,
Stopping with a silence of sea grass, a silence of prairie corn.
Hats: tell me your high hopes.

UNDER A HAT RIM

While the hum and the hurry
Of passing footfalls
Beat in my ear like the restless surf
Of a wind-blown sea,
A soul came to me
Out of the look on a face.

Eyes like a lake
Where a storm-wind roams
Caught me from under
The rim of a hat.
  I thought of a midsea wreck
  and bruised fingers clinging
  to a broken stateroom door.

HITS AND RUNS

I remember the Chillicothe ball players
   grappling the Rock Island ball players
   in a sixteen-inning game ended by darkness.
And the shoulders of the Chillicothe players
   were a red smoke against the sundown
   and the shoulders of the Rock Island players
   were a yellow smoke against the sundown.
And the umpire's voice was hoarse
   calling balls and strikes and outs
   and the umpire's throat fought in the dust
   for a song.

I remember black winter waters,
I remember thin white birches,
I remember sleepy twilight hills,
I remember riding across New
Hampshire lengthways.
I remember a station named
"Halcyon," a brakeman call-
ing to passengers "Halcyon!!
Halcyon!!"
I remember having heard the
gold diggers dig out only
enough for wedding rings.
I remember a stately child tell-
ing me her father gets letters
addressed "Robert Frost, New
Hampshire."
I remember an old Irish saying,
"His face is like a fiddle and
every one who sees him must
love him."
I have one remember, two re-
members, ten remembers; I
have a little handkerchief
bundle of remembers.

One early evening star just over
a cradle moon,

One dark river with a spatter of
later stars caught,
One funnel of a motorcar headlight up a hill,
One team of horses hauling a
bobsled load of wood,
One boy on skis picking himself
up after a tumble—
I remember one and a one and a
one riding across New Hampshire lengthways: I have a little handkerchief bundle of remembers.

NIAGARA
from *The People, Yes*

The tumblers of the rapids go white, go green,
go changing over the gray, the brown, the rocks.
The fight of the water, the stones,
the fight makes a foam laughter
before the last look over the long slide
down the spread of a sheen in the straight fall.
    Then the growl, the chutter,
    down under the boom and the muffle,
    the hoo hoi deep,
    the hoo hoi down,
        this is Niagara.

CHEAP BLUE

Hill blue among the leaves in summer,
Hill blue among the branches in winter—
Light sea blue at the sand beaches in winter,
Deep sea blue in the deep deep waters—
Prairie blue, mountain blue—
    Who can pick a pocketful of these blues,
      a handkerchief of these blues,
    And go walking, talking, walking as though
    God gave them a lot of loose change
    For spending money, to throw at the birds,
    To flip into the tin cups of blind men?

MOTHER AND CHILD
from *The People, Yes*

"I love you,"
said a great mother.
"I love you for what you are
knowing so well what you are.
And I love you more yet, child,
deeper yet than ever, child,
for what you are going to be,
knowing so well you are going far,
knowing your great works are ahead,
ahead and beyond,
yonder and far over yet."

CORN BELT

IMPROVED FARM LAND

Tall timber stood here once,
   here on a corn belt farm along the Monon.
Here the roots of a half mile of trees
    dug their runners deep in the loam
    for a grip and a hold against windstorms.
Then the axmen came and the chips flew
    to the zing of steel and handle—
    the lank railsplitters cut the big ones first,
    the beeches and the oaks, then the brush.
Dynamite, wagons and horses took the stumps—
    the plows sunk their teeth in—
    now it is first-class corn land—improved property—
    and the hogs grunt over the fodder crops.
It would come hard now for this half mile of improved farm
     land
    along the Monon corn belt,
    on a piece of Grand Prairie,
    to remember once it had a great singing family of trees.

PLOWBOY

After the last red sunset glimmer,
Black on the line of a low hill rise,
Formed into moving shadows, I saw
A plowboy and two horses lined against the gray,
Plowing in the dusk the last furrow.
The turf had a gleam of brown,
And smell of soil was in the air,
And, cool and moist, a haze of April.

I shall remember you long,
Plowboy and horses against the sky in shadow.
I shall remember you and the picture
You made for me,
Turning the turf in the dusk
And haze of an April gloaming.

1908

FROG SONGS

The silver burbles of the frogs wind and swirl.
The lines of their prongs swing up in a spray.
They cut the air with bird line curves.
The eye sees nothing, the ear is filled, the head remembers
The beat of the swirl of frog throat silver prongs
In the early springtime when eggs open, when feet learn,
When the crying of the water begins a new year.

Open the barn door, farm woman,
It is time for the cows to be milked.
Their udders are full from the sleep night.
Open the door with your right hand shuttling a cleat,
Your left hand pulling a handle.
The smell of the barn is let out to the pastures.
Dawn lets itself in at the open door.
A cow let out in the barnyard all the night
Looks on as though you do this every morning.
Open the barn door, farm woman, you do it
As you have done it five hundred times.
As a sleep woman heavy with the earth,
Clean as a milk pail washed in the sun,
You open the barn door a half mile away
And a cow almost turns its head and looks on.

SUMMER MORNING
from *Prairie*

A wagonload of radishes on a summer morning.
Sprinkles of dew on the crimson-purple balls.
The farmer on the seat dangles the reins
    on the rumps of dapple-gray horses.
The farmer's daughter with a basket of eggs
    dreams of a new hat to wear to the county fair.

1911

The time of the brown gold comes softly.
Oat shocks are alive in brown gold belts,
    the short and the shambling oat shocks
    sit on the stubble and straw.
The timothy hay, the fodder corn, the cabbage
    and the potatoes, across their leaves are
    footsteps.
There is a bold green up over the cracks in
    the corn rows where the crickets go criss-
    cross errands, where the bugs carry pack-
    ages.
Flutter and whirr, you birdies, you newcomers
    in lines and sashes, tellers of harvest
    weather on the way, belts of brown gold
    coming softly.
It is very well the old-time streamers take
    up the old-time gold haze against the west-
    ern timber line.
It is the old time again when months and birds
    tell each other, "Oh, very well," and repeat it
    where the fields and the timber lines meet
    in belts of brown gold hazes, "Oh, very
    well, Oh, very well."

The wind blows.
The corn leans.
The corn leaves go rustling.
    The march time and the windbeat
    are on October drums.
    The stalks of fodder bend all one way,
    the way the last windstorm passed.

"Put on my winter clothes;
get me an ulster—a yellow ulster—
to lay down in in January
and shut my eyes
and cover my ears
in snowdrifts."

The wind blows.
The corn leans.
The fodder is russet.
    October says to the leaves,
    "Rustle now to the last lap,
    to the last leg of the year."

CORNHUSKERS

The frost loosens cornhusks.
The sun, the rain, the wind
    loosen cornhusks.
The men and women are helpers.
They are all cornhuskers together.
I see them late in the western evening
    in a smoke-red dust.

HAYSTACKS

After the sunburn of the day
handling a pitchfork at a hayrack,
after the eggs and biscuit and coffee,
the pearl-gray haystacks
in the gloaming
are cool prayers
to the harvest hands.

HARVEST SUNSET

Red gold of pools,
Sunset furrows six o'clock,
And the farmer done in the fields
And the cows in the barns with bulging udders.

Take the cows and the farmer,
Take the barns and bulging udders.
Leave the red gold of pools
And sunset furrows six o'clock.
The farmer's wife is singing.
The farmer's boy is whistling.
I wash my hands in red gold of pools.

PRAIRIE BARN
from *The People, Yes*

For sixty years the pine lumber barn
had held cows, horses, hay, harness, tools, junk,
amid the prairie winds of Knox County, Illinois
and the corn crops came and went, plows and wagons,
and hands milked, hands husked and harnessed
and held the leather reins of horse teams
in dust and dog days, in late fall sleet
till the work was done that fall.
And the barn was a witness, stood and saw it all.
      "That old barn on your place, Charlie,
      was nearly falling last time I saw it,
      how is it now?"
      "I got some poles to hold it on the east side
      and the wind holds it up on the west."

LIMITED CROSSING WISCONSIN
from *Prairie*

A headlight searches a snowstorm.
A funnel of white light shoots from over the pilot
    of the Pioneer Limited crossing Wisconsin.

In the morning hours, in the dawn,
The sun puts out the stars of the sky
And the headlight of the Limited train.

The fireman waves his hand
    to a country school teacher on a bobsled.
A boy, yellow hair, red scarf and mittens,
    on the bobsled, in his lunch box
    a pork chop sandwich and a V of gooseberry pie.

The horses fathom a snow to their knees.
Snow hats are on the rolling prairie hills.
The Mississippi bluffs wear snow hats.

SONGS
from *Prairie*

When the morning sun is on the trumpet-vine blossoms,
 Sing at the kitchen pans:
 Shout All Over God's Heaven.
When the rain slants on the potato hills
And the sun plays a silver shaft on the last shower,
 Sing to the bush at the backyard fence:
 Mighty Lak a Rose.
When the icy sleet pounds on the storm windows
And the house lifts to a great breath,
 Sing for the outside hills:
 The Ole Sheep Done Know the Road,
 the Young Lambs Must Find the Way.

The top of the ridge is a cornfield.
It rests all winter under snow.
It feeds the broken snowdrifts in spring
To a clear stream cutting down hill to the river.
Late in summer the stream dries; rabbits run and
　　birds hop along the dry mud bottom.
Fall time comes and it fills with leaves; oaks and
　　shagbark hickories drop their summer hats,
　　ribbons, handkerchiefs.
"This is how I keep warm all winter," the stream
　　murmurs, waiting till the snowdrifts melt and
　　the ice loosens and the clear singing babble
　　of spring comes back.

NIGHT

NIGHT
from *The Windy City*

Night gathers itself into a ball of dark yarn.
Night loosens the ball and it spreads.
The lookouts from the shores of Lake Michigan
    find night follows day,
      and ping! ping! across sheet gray
      the boat lights put their signals.
Night lets the dark yarn unravel,
Night speaks and the yarns change
    to fog and blue strands.

Chatter of birds two by two
raises a night song
joining a litany of running water—
sheer waters showing the russet of old stones
remembering many rains.

And the long willows drowse
on the shoulders of the running water,
and sleep from much music;
joined songs of day-end,
feathery throats and stony waters,
in a choir chanting new psalms.

It is too much for the long willows
when low laughter of a red moon comes down;
and the willows drowse and sleep
on the shoulders of the running water.

TIMBER MOON

There is a way the moon looks into the timber at night
And tells the walnut trees secrets of silver sand—
There is a way the moon makes a lattice work
Under the leaves of the hazel bushes—
There is a way the moon understands the hoot owl
Sitting on an arm of a sugar maple throwing its
One long lonesome cry up the ladders of the moon—
There is a way the moon finds company early in the fall
      time.

NIGHT TOO HAS NUMBERS
from *The People, Yes*

In the long flat panhandle of Texas
far off on the grassland of the cattle country
near noon they sight a rider coming toward them
and the sky may be a cold neverchanging gray
or the sky may be changing its numbers
back and forth all day even and odd numbers
and the afternoon slides away somewhere
and they see their rider is alive yet
their rider is coming nearer yet
and they expect what happens and it happens again
he and his horse ride in late for supper
yet not too late
and night is on and the stars are out
and night too slides away somewhere
night too has even and odd numbers.

RIVER MOONS

The double moon,
    one on the high backdrop of the west,
    one on the curve of the river face,
The sky moon of fire
and the river moon of water,
    I am taking these home in a basket
    hung on an elbow,
    such a teeny-weeny elbow,
    in my head.
I saw them last night,
    a cradle moon, two horns of a moon,
    such an early hopeful moon,
    such a child's moon
    for all young hearts
    to make a picture of.
The river—I remember this like a picture—
    the river was the upper twist
    of a written question mark.
I know now it takes
    many many years to write a river,
    a twist of water asking a question.
And white stars moved when the moon moved,
    and one red star kept burning,
    and the Big Dipper was almost overhead.

SLEEP IMPRESSION

The dark blue wind
ran on the early autumn sky
in the fields of yellow moon harvest.
  I slept, I almost slept,
  I said listening:
Trees you have leaves rustling like rain
  when there is no rain.

NOCTURNE IN A DESERTED BRICKYARD

Stuff of the moon
Runs on the lapping sand
Out to the longest shadows.
Under the curving willows,
And round the creep of the wave line,
Fluxions of yellow and dusk on the waters
Make a wide dreaming pansy of an old pond in the night.

BETWEEN TWO HILLS

Between two hills
The old town stands.
The houses loom
And the roofs and trees
And the dusk and the dark,
The damp and the dew
   Are there.

The prayers are said
And the people rest
For sleep is there
And the touch of dreams
   Is over all.

WINDOW

Night from a railroad car window
Is a great, dark, soft thing
Broken across with slashes of light.

PODS

Pea pods cling to stems.
Neponset, the village,
Clings to the Burlington railway main line.
Terrible midnight limiteds roar through
Hauling sleepers to the Rockies and Sierras.
The earth is slightly shaken
And Neponset trembles slightly in its sleep.

DROWSY

Sleep is the gift of many spiders
The webs tie down the sleepers easy.

SHEEP

Thousands of sheep, soft-footed, black-nosed sheep—
one by one going up the hill and over the fence—
one by one four-footed pattering up and over—
one by one wiggling their stub tails as they take
    the short jump and go over—
one by one silently unless for the multitudinous drumming
    of their hoofs as they move on and go over—
thousands and thousands of them in the gray haze of evening
    just after sundown—
one by one slanting in a long line to pass over the hill—

I am the slow, long-legged Sleepyman and I love you sheep
    in Persia, California, Argentina, Australia, or Spain—
you are the thoughts that help me when I, the Sleepyman,
lay my hands on the eyelids of the children of the world
    at eight o'clock every night—
you thousands and thousands of sheep in a procession of dusk
making an endless multitudinous drumming on the hills
    with your hoofs.

BLOSSOM THEMES

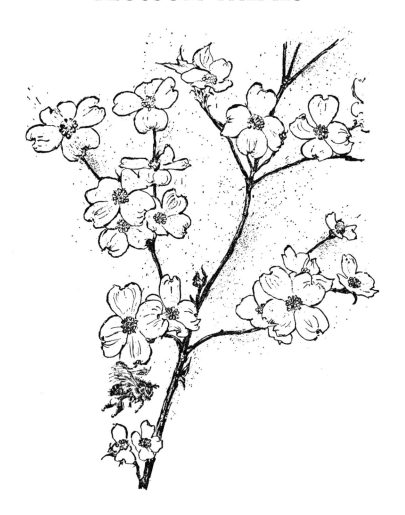

BLOSSOM THEMES

1

Late in the winter came one day
When there was a whiff on the wind,
a suspicion, a cry not to be heard
    of perhaps blossoms, perhaps green
    grass and clean hills lifting roll-
    ing shoulders.
Does the nose get the cry of spring
    first of all? is the nose thankful
    and thrilled first of all?

2

If the blossoms come down
so they must fall on snow
because spring comes this year
before winter is gone,
then both snow and blossoms look sad;
peaches, cherries, the red summer apples,
all say it is a hard year.
The wind has its own way of picking off
the smell of peach blossoms and then
carrying that smell miles and miles.
    Women washing dishes in lonely farmhouses
    stand at the door and say, "Something is
    happening."

A little foam of the summer sea
of blossoms,
a foam finger of white leaves,
shut these away—
high into the summer wind runners.
Let the wind be white too.

GRASSROOTS

Grass clutches at the dark dirt with finger holds.
Let it be blue grass, barley, rye or wheat,
Let it be button weed or butter-and-eggs,
Let it be Johnny-jump-ups springing clean blue streaks.
Grassroots down under put fingers into dark dirt.

LANDSCAPE

See the trees lean to the wind's way of learning.
See the dirt of the hills shape to the water's
    way of learning.
See the lift of it all go the way the biggest
    wind and the strongest water want it.

LITTLE SKETCH

There are forked branches of trees
Where the leaves shudder obediently,
Where the hangover leaves
Flow in a curve downward;
And between the forks and leaves,
In patches and angles, in square handfuls,
The orange lights of the done sunset
Come and filter and pour.

FLOWERS TELL MONTHS

Gold buttons in the garden today—
Among the brown-eyed susans the golden spiders are
    gamboling.
The blue sisters of the white asters speak to each other.

After the travel of the snows—
Buttercups come in a yellow rain,
Johnny-jump-ups in a blue mist—
Wild azaleas with a low spring cry.

CRISSCROSS

Spring crosses over into summer.
This is as it always was.

Buds on the redhaw, beetles in the loam,
And the interference of the green leaves
At the blue roofs of the spring sky
Crossing over into summer—
These are ways, this is out and on.
This always was.

The tumble out and the push up,
The breaking of the little doors,
The look again at the mother sun,
The feel of the blue roofs over—
This is summer? This always was?

The whispering sprigs of buds stay put.
The spiders are after the beetles.
The farmer is driving a tractor turning furrows.
The hired man drives a manure spreader.
The oven bird hops in dry leaves.
The woodpecker beats his tattoo.
Is this it? Is spring crossing over?
Is it summer? And this always was?
The whispering pinks, the buds on the redhaw,
The blue roofs of the sky . . . stay put.

SUMMER GRASS

Summer grass aches and whispers.

It wants something;
it calls out and sings;
it pours out wishes to the overhead stars.

The rain hears;
the rain answers;
the rain is slow coming;
the rain wets the face of the grass.

Let the crows go by hawking their caw and caw.
They have been swimming in midnights of coal mines some-
    where.
Let 'em hawk their caw and caw.

Let the woodpecker drum and drum on a hickory stump.
He has been swimming in red and blue pools somewhere
    hundreds of years
And the blue has gone to his wings and the red has gone to
    his head.
Let his red head drum and drum.

Let the dark pools hold the birds in a looking-glass.
And if the pool wishes, let it shiver to the blur of many
    wings, old swimmers from old places.

Let the redwing streak a line of vermilion on the green
    wood lines.
And the mist along the river fix its purple in lines of a
    woman's shawl on lazy shoulders.

ON A RAILROAD RIGHT OF WAY

Stream, go hide yourself.
In the tall grass, in the cat-tails,
In the browns of autumn, the last purple
    asters, the yellow whispers.
On the moss rock levels leave the marks
    of your wave-lengths.
Sing in your gravel, in your clean gully.
Let the moaning railroad trains go by.
Till they stop you, go on with your song.

The minnies spin in the water gravel,
In the spears of the early autumn sun.
There must be winter fish.
Babies, you will be jumping fish
In the first snow month.

CRABAPPLES

Sweeten these bitter wild crabapples,
  Illinois October sun.
The roots here came from the wilderness,
  came before man came here.
They are bitter as the wild is bitter.

Give these crabapples your softening gold,
  October sun.
Go through to the white wet seeds inside
  and soften them black.
Make these bitter apples sweet.
They want you, sun.

        The drop and the fall,
        the drop and the fall,
        the apples leaving the branches
        for the black earth under,
        they know you from last year,
        the year before last year,
        October sun.

HAZE GOLD

Sun, you may send your haze gold
Filling the fall afternoon
With a flimmer of many gold feathers.
Leaves, you may linger in the fall sunset
Like late lingering butterflies before frost.
Treetops, you may sift the sunset cross-lights
Spreading a loose checkerwork of gold and shadow.
Winter comes soon—shall we save this, lay it by,
Keep all we can of these haze gold yellows?

WINTER GOLD

The same gold of summer was on the winter hills,
the oat straw gold, the gold of slow sun change.

The stubble was chilly and lonesome,
the stub feet clomb up the hills and stood.

The flat cry of one wheeling crow faded and came,
ran on the stub gold flats and faded and came.

Fade-me, find-me, slow lights rang their changes
on the flats of oat straw gold on winter hills.

WIND, SEA, AND SKY

WINDS OF THE WINDY CITY
from *The Windy City*

Winds of the Windy City,
    come out of the prairie,
    all the way from Medicine Hat.
    Come out of the inland sea blue water,
    come where they nickname a city for you.

Corn wind in the fall,
    come off the black lands,
    come off the whisper of the silk hangers,
    the lap of the flat spear leaves.

Blue water wind in summer,
    come off the blue miles of lake,
    carry your inland sea blue fingers,
    carry us cool,
    carry your blue to our homes.

White spring winds,
    come off the bag wool clouds,
    come off the running melted snow,
    come white as the arms of snow-born children.

Gray fighting winter winds,
    come along on the tearing blizzard tails,

the snouts of the hungry hunting storms,
come fighting gray in winter.

Winds of the Windy City,
Winds of corn and sea blue,
Spring wind white
    and fighting winter gray,
Come home here—
    they nickname a city for you.

CHILDREN OF THE WIND
from *The People, Yes*

On the shores of Lake Michigan
high on a wooden pole, in a box,
two purple martins had a home
and taken away down to Martinique
and let loose, they flew home,
thousands of miles to be home again.
    And this has lights of wonder
    echo and pace and echo again.
The birds let out began flying
north north-by-west north
till they were back home.
How their instruments told them
of ceiling, temperature, air pressure,
how their control-boards gave them
reports of fuel, ignition, speeds,
is out of the record, out.

Across spaces of sun and cloud,
in rain and fog, through air pockets,
wind with them, wind against them,
stopping for subsistence rations,
whirling in gust and spiral,
these people of the air,
these children of the wind,
had a sense of where to go and how,
how to go north north-by-west north,
till they came to one wooden pole,
till they were home again.

DOCKS

Strolling along
By the teeming docks,
I watch the ships put out.
Black ships that heave and lunge
And move like mastodons
Arising from lethargic sleep.

The fathomed harbor
Calls them not nor dares
Them to a strain of action,
But outward, on and outward,
Sounding low-reverberating calls,
Shaggy in the half-lit distance,
They pass the pointed headland,
View the wide, far-lifting wilderness
And leap with cumulative speed
To test the challenge of the sea.

Plunging,
Doggedly onward plunging,
Into salt and mist and foam and sun.

FROM THE SHORE

A lone gray bird,
Dim-dipping, far-flying,
Alone in the shadows and grandeurs and tumults
Of night and the sea
And the stars and storms.

Out over the darkness it wavers and hovers,
Out into the gloom it swings and batters,
Out into the wind and the rain and the vast,
Out into the pit of a great black world,
Where fogs are at battle, sky-driven, sea-blown,
Love of mist and rapture of flight,
Glories of chance and hazards of death
On its eager and palpitant wings.

Out into the deep of the great dark world,
Beyond the long borders where foam and drift
Of the sundering waves are lost and gone
On the tides that plunge and rear and crumble.

FLUX

Sand of the sea runs red
Where the sunset reaches and quivers.
Sand of the sea runs yellow
Where the moon slants and wavers.

SKY PRAYERS
from *Good Morning, America*

Sea sunsets, give us keepsakes.
Prairie gloamings, pay us for prayers.
Mountain clouds on bronze skies—
   Give us great memories.
Let us have summer roses.
Let us have tawny harvest haze in pumpkin time.
Let us have springtime faces to toil for and play for.
Let us have the fun of booming winds on long waters.
Give us dreamy blue twilights—
   of winter evenings—
   to wrap us in a coat of dreaminess.
Moonlight, come down—shine down, moonlight—
   meet every bird cry and every song
   calling to a hard old earth,
   a sweet young earth.

ROLLING CLOUDS
from *Sky Talk*

Wool white horses and their heads sag and roll,
Snow white sheep and their tails drag far,
Impossible animals ever more impossible—
    They walk on the sky to say How do you do?
        Or Good-by or Back-soon-maybe.

Or would you say any white flowers come
    more lovely than certain white clouds?
Or would you say any tall mountains beckon,
    rise and beckon beyond certain tall walking clouds?

Is there any roll of white sea-horses equal to
    the sky-horse white of certain clouds rolling?

BABY SONG OF THE FOUR WINDS

Let me be your baby, south wind.
Rock me, let me rock, rock me now.
Rock me low, rock me warm.
Let me be your baby.

Comb my hair, west wind.
Comb me with a cowlick.
Or let me go with a pompadour.
Come on, west wind, make me your baby.

North wind, shake me where I'm foolish.
Shake me loose and change my ways.
Cool my ears with a blue sea wind.
I'm your baby, make me behave.

And you, east wind, what can I ask?
A fog comfort? A fog to tuck me in?
Fix me so and let me sleep.
I'm your baby—and I always was.

BROKEN SKY

The sky of gray is eaten in six places,
Rag holes stand out.
It is an army blanket and the sleeper
  slept too near the fire.

SANTA FE SKETCH

The valley was swept with a blue broom to the west.

And to the west, on the fringes of a mesa sunset,
there are blue broom leavings, hangover blue wisps—
bluer than the blue floor the broom touched
before and after it caught the blue sweepings.

The valley was swept with a blue broom to the west.

SILVER POINT

The silver point of an evening star
dropping toward the hammock of new moon
 over Lake Okoboji,
  over prairie waters in Iowa—
it was framed in the lights
 just after twilight.

Long ago I learned how to sleep,
In an old apple orchard where the wind swept by counting
  its money and throwing it away,
In a wind-gaunt orchard where the limbs forked out and lis-
  tened or never listened at all,
In a passel of trees where the branches trapped the wind into
  whistling, "Who, who are you?"
I slept with my head in an elbow on a summer afternoon
  and there I took a sleep lesson.
There I went away saying: I know why they sleep, I know
  how they trap the tricky winds.
Long ago I learned how to listen to the singing wind and
  how to forget and how to hear the deep whine,
Slapping and lapsing under the day blue and the night stars:
      Who, who are you?

        Who can ever forget
        listening to the wind go by
        counting its money
        and throwing it away?